CRONES DON'T WHINE

OTHER BOOKS BY JEAN SHINODA BOLEN, MD

The Tao of Psychology

Goddesses in Everywoman

Gods in Everyman

Ring of Power

Crossing to Avalon

Close to the Bone

The Millionth Circle

Goddesses in Older Women

JEAN SHINODA BOLEN, MD

CRONES
DON'T WHINE

Concentrated Wisdom
for Mature Women

Conari Press

Cover Design: Lisa Levart
Layout & Design: Maxine Ressler & Elina Diaz
Cover Photograph: Lush Photography

For permission requests, please contact the publisher at:
Mango Publishing Group
2850 S Douglas Road, 2nd Floor
Coral Gables, FL 33134 USA
info@mango.bz

For special orders, quantity sales, course adoptions and corporate sales, please
email the publisher at sales@mango.bz. For trade and wholesale sales, please
contact Ingram Publisher Services at customer.service@ingramcontent.com or
+1.800.509.4887.

Crones Don't Whine: Concentrated Wisdom for Mature Women

Library of Congress Cataloging-in-Publication Data: 2023952621
ISBN: (pb) 978-1-68481-486-2, (e) 978-1-68481-487-9
BISAC: OCC019000, BODY, MIND & SPIRIT / Inspiration &
Personal Growth

*The third aspect of the ancient Triple Goddess
was the Crone.
The third phase of a woman's life is after menopause.*

*To aspire to be a crone
is to want the psychological and spiritual growth
that she symbolizes.*

*The crone is an archetype
an inner potential that we grow into
becoming.*

CONTENTS

Possibilities and Thoughts   85

Crones Don't Whine Resource Guide 111

Selected Bibliography   137

PREFACE

Among us, there are young Crones and old Crones. It's not about age or even about gender, it's about wise old souls who come back into the world as infants with no memory of past lives, and yet seem to be interested and taking in wherever they are. In infancy, it could be a baby who seems to be looking around with open eyes. Often as they grow older and as they enter new situations, it's natural for them to trust who is there and to sense warmth or not. Regardless of the situation even when young, "Crones Don't Whine."

In family situations where there is chaos or emotional outbursts because the parent or parents are immature, angry, or intoxicated, their young children may behave like them; except perhaps if there is a quiet child in the family who doesn't make a fuss while their siblings take after their parents. One parent may cry and wail. Another might be angry and throw things. An exceptional child in such a family tends to be quietly paying attention and behaving, just as children in stable families often are. Curiosity, learning, and aspirations are typically part of the lives of these children as they grow older. Oftentimes they are wise to keep thoughts and dreams to themselves.

Entering graduate and professional schools, individual women typically get along with peers and authorities, which was my experience. Women continue to do so as they age, many even if they were initially looked down upon because of gender, race, or class; and as they excelled in school, respect grew. After the mid-twentieth century, college educated women began to enter education, law, medicine, and business; later, into technology and science; and recently, into politics, religion, and government. I sense that men who are wise, competent, and responsible with loving feelings will one day feel honored to be called a Crone.

1

A NEW PERSPECTIVE ON
THE "CRONE" WORD

A New Perspective on the "Crone" Word

THERE IS A MEDIEVAL SOUND to the word "crone" and a mischievous note to the suggestion that a woman would aspire to be one. It's not what any of us aspired to be in our youth, but that was when an older woman never told her true age, and before women came into their own as people in their own right or lived as long as we now do. We of the Women's Movement generation or its subsequent beneficiaries continue to have opportunities that never existed for all the generations (as far back as the ancient Greeks) that preceded us. We have been reinventing ourselves at each stage of life. I am proposing that it is time to reclaim and redefine "crone" from the word pile of disparaging names to call older women, and to make becoming a "crone" a crowning inner achievement of the third phase of life.

To be a crone is about inner development, not outer appearance. A crone is a woman who has wisdom, compassion, humor, courage, and vitality. She has a sense of truly being herself, can express what she knows and feels, and take action when need be. She does not avert her eyes or numb her mind from reality. She can see the flaws and imperfections in herself and others, but the light in which she sees is not harsh and judgmental. She has learned to trust herself to know what she knows.

These crone qualities are not acquired overnight. One does not become a full-fledged crone automatically following menopause, any more than growing older *and* wiser go hand in hand. There are decades that follow menopause in which to grow psychologically and spiritually.

Crones don't whine is a fundamental characterization. It's a basic "rule" that describes conduct unbecoming of a crone. Whining is an attitude that blocks spiritual and psychological development. Whining makes genuine communication impossible and extorts what then cannot be freely given. To catch oneself whining is an "aha!" moment. This insight can be the beginning of wisdom for a whiner who has the ability to observe herself and wants to change.

While an ordinary mirror reflects surface appearances, descriptive words can be mirrors in which we see intangible qualities having to do with soul. Each of the thirteen chapters that follow in the next section focuses on such qualities, specifically those that are characteristic of juicy, wise women. It is in cultivating these qualities that the third phase of life becomes a culmination time for inner beauty and wisdom. It is the perspective that makes the prime years of this phase of life an especially rich time to enjoy who we are, what we have, and what we are doing. It is a time when wisdom calls upon us to use our time, energy, and vitality well. It is an opportunity to have more chances, experience shifts in roles, and develop talents and interests. This may be a time to play and express affection, or a time for creativity or sensuality, or a time for meditation or therapy, or a time for family or a time when family recedes, or a time to make a difference in the world.

Crones can make a difference. What you say and do can change a dysfunctional family pattern. Your mentoring can support and make it possible for another to grow and blossom. You can be a healing influence for good. You can have a ripple effect throughout generations to come or through institutions and communities. With vision and intention, and in numbers and influence, crones together can change the world.

While this was written with women in the prime post menopausal years of life in mind, if you glean something from reading this earlier in life, so much the better! So listen up, precrones! Also, while men are handicapped by socialization and physiology, exceptional men can be crones.

10

It's a wise woman who reads the thirteen qualities and is amused to realize that she can see herself and the idea of being a crone, or becoming one, in a positive light. It is an evolving woman who sees in any of one or more of these qualities what she wants to develop in herself and finds in these words support to do so.

A lifetime is the material that each of us has to work with. Until this span is over, we are all still *in process,* in the midst of an unfinished story. What we do with our lives is our *magnum opus,* or great work of personal creativity. If we acquire a crone's-eye view, then we will see ourselves and others from the perspective of soul rather than ego. Aging well is a goal worth wanting.

A Word About
the Use of the Word

In the following pages, I often describe women as crones, or speak of an inner crone or a crone archetype. Sometimes I use crone and wisewoman interchangeably. In women's psyches and in my words, you will find ambiguity, a blurring of distinctions. Sometimes, in some situations, a woman is a wise crone, and a moment later, she is not.

Sometimes, archetype and woman are one in the same. Sometimes, crone wisdom fleetingly comes to mind and is ignored. This is so because the inner or archetypal crone is a latent presence in everyone's psyche, in men and even in children. The crone does not shout over a din of competing parts of the personality. The crone is a potential, much like an inherent talent, that needs to be recognized and practiced in order to develop. This wise presence in your psyche will grow, once you trust that there is a crone within and begin to listen. Then in the quiet of your own mind, pay attention to her perceptions and intuitions and act upon them.

Crone qualities are the distinguishing features by which a crone (as a woman or an archetype) can be known.

THE THIRTEEN QUALITIES

2

1

CRONES DON'T WHINE

TO BE A CRONE, you need to let go of what should have been, could have been, might have been. You need to silence the whining in your head that will come out of your mouth next. Whining makes you unable to live in the present, or be good company for anyone—even yourself. Whiners assume they were and are entitled to a different life from the one they have. Whiners do not see that everyone has had a share of the bad things that happen to people. Ungrateful for what they do have, whiners cannot enjoy the present.

Juicy Older Woman Rule #1.
Crones don't whine.

What was, was. What is, is. Plain and simple. You may have gotten the idea that you were supposed to marry and live happily ever after, have had perfect children, and (since the Women's Movement) also have had the perfect career. And here you are. Whatever happened or didn't happen before now is what was. You can't live it over. The past is the past. Menopause marks the end of the childbearing years. This and other realities are what *is*.

Grief is not whining. Even whimpering is not whining. Maybe some body part is not working well or is painful—and you are doing what can be done, medically and otherwise. You may have financial limitations. Whatever it is that you are struggling with can be told to people who need to know, want to know, or as updates to friends with whom you share the ongoing story of your life. However, crones don't bore others with a litany of their symptoms—organ recitals or tales of woe—that have an air of performance or bragging. A crone knows she and her troubles are not the center of the universe and knows other people have problems, too. A crone doesn't indulge whining children, or whining inner children. Especially her own.

A whining child is a wheedling one: she wants something that is not going to be freely given. What she wants may not be good for her (whatever it is that the whining child in the supermarket wants her tired mother to buy for her, for example). When she gets it, satisfaction is fleeting. It was another small act of extortion and appeasement.

Older women who are not crones might not whine and wheedle outright or tug on you physically like a child in the market. But emotional extortion and appeasement, fleeting satisfactions, and general unhappiness are the same pervasive patterns. The tugs are emotional ones: need, entitlement, suffering, justification, a tone and energy conveyed and felt through the voice. Conversations with a whiner are depleting. Other people feel trapped and respond insincerely, stay away, and feel guilty.

Change begins with insight. If you recognize yourself in this description or are considering the possibility it may fit, you can do so in the privacy of your mind. An honest appraisal is not an accusation; it is a working diagnosis, a starting point to help you with unhappiness. Are you feeling sorry for yourself? Have you fallen into a state of "poor me" resentment? Have you lost your sense of proportion? If so, what might be your equivalent of, "I cried because I had no shoes, and then I met a man who had no feet"?

As we grow older, especially if we are outer-directed, it is not difficult to find more and more to whine about. This poses a risk of a negative transformation into the archetypal martyr-mother (a woman who is one now, was not always so, after all). With perspective, humor, and wisdom, however, the potential to whine that is in us all when we might want other than what we have, doesn't take us over.

My friend Jananne, who heard me say that "crones don't whine," laughingly told me how she resisted the temptation to call me up and whine when confronted with the daunting task of unpacking and beginning a new life. Instead, she play-acted an exaggerated version of her whiner, with just herself as the audience, and then kept on with what had to be done. This is the same friend who caught me complaining and made up a song, "piss and moan and bitch, piss and moan and bitch, piss and moan and bitch and groan" to the tune of the folk dance, "Put your little foot, put your little foot, put your little foot right down . . ."

One whining variation is expressed as acerbic wit or sarcasm directed toward a person (often an "ex") or an institution. At first, it seems very different from outright whining and then the similarities begin to show. The past is continually injected into conversations in this way. Friends try to change the subject when they can, preferring not to be a captive audience to the latest insight or outrage. Like the outright whiner, she is not able to let go of what *was* or accept what *is*.

Some whiners lie awake at night, going through reruns of past incidents in which they felt poorly treated. This can become a time to wrestle with letting the matter go, if only to get some sleep. If such is the case, there is something you can do until you fall asleep. It will also be a means to hear the crone. Just breathe slowly and pay attention to your breath. Listen to words the crone would say to you (as you say or think them to yourself) and then listen to what she says about herself.

Breathe in. *That was then.*

Breathe out. *This is now.*

Breathe in. *I am.*

Breathe out. *Peace.*

The inner crone has an observing eye and sensitive ear. Once you know her, she will catch you whining or feeling sorry for yourself. Once caught, the jig is up; whining is conduct unbecoming a crone.

2

CRONES ARE JUICY

A CRONE IS A JUICY older woman with zest, passions, and soul. If you aspire to be one, the secret is to be yourself, while your mind, heart, and body still function well enough, and you appreciate being alive. Metaphorically, the three phases of the moon—waxing, full, and waning— the three phases of the ancient goddess—maiden, mother, crone—and the three biological markers of menarche, menstruation, and menopause divide women's lives into a three-act play. This is Act 3. The curtain will come down at the end of it. In Act 3, you may pick up on threads of meaning from earlier phases of your life and find yourself absorbed in something new. There are completions and endings; doors close and others open. Whatever the particulars, what makes life juicy is being deeply involved in life.

You may be a juicy crone who discovered how delicious solitude is, with a place and life of your own, and only yourself to please. You may be a juicy crone whose hearth and heart are welcoming of numerous people, whose life might even be a center of activity for a community. You may be a juicy crone who found a younger lover. You may be married to the right person ("right" according to who you are and what you want in your life). You may be seeing the world as a tourist, pilgrim, or Peace Corps volunteer. You may be reading and learning what you are interested in knowing. You may be an activist working at making a part of the world better. You may be in a creative phase of your life. You may love spending time with grandchildren, or not (depending upon who they are as much as who you are).

Others—including your grown children—may think that you are inappropriate, whimsical, or eccentric because you are able to be authentic and are not conforming to a stereotype they have of "a proper woman of your age." Or you may find yourself unexpectedly being a role model for women younger than yourself, whose mothers fit the stereotype.

When I wrote *Goddesses in Older Women: Archetypes in Women Over Fifty*, I was very much aware that *crone* was not an acceptable mainstream word for women over fifty. *Juicy crone*, however, struck a chord. The juxtaposition of these two words seemed both a contradiction in terms and a welcomed possibility; "dried up and old" were after all, the more usual adjectives attached to "crone."

Juicy brings to mind metaphors to do with moisture and electricity. In American slang, the positive meaning of "juice" implies being plugged into a source of power or energy, or having the ability to make things happen. The juice that truly vitalizes us is unconditional love, which is the one source of energy that is never depleted; to the contrary, the more we give away, the more there is.

In nature, vitality—being alive—means that there is a source of water to nurture new growth and sustain life, which is moist. For both physical health and emotional well-being, metaphoric moisture and flow are also essential. Genuine feelings and unblocked expression of them are moist. In grief, tears of sorrow flow. In uninhibited laughter and joy, tears flow. To be involved and engaged in life is a juicy proposition. Every juicy crone taps into a wellspring or a deep aquifer of meaning in her psyche.

3

CRONES HAVE GREEN THUMBS

IF YOU ARE A JUICY CRONE, you may not be a gardener, but you do have a green thumb. Crones are in the generative phase of life, a time of fostering growth. Plants and people respond to crones with green thumbs. (As might the planet itself, if a critical number of crones would take on this job.) Crones nurture growth. Crones weed well. Crones prune. Crones know that different plants and people need different conditions in order to thrive. Crones protect what is vulnerable until survival on its own is possible. Crones have learned patience. Crones can wait as the seasons turn. Crones know that something small can grow big, that something can bloom or bear fruit before it dies.

Gardening is a metaphor. It is also what you may actually do. Working with your hands, digging in the soil to prepare the ground for starter plants or seeds, feeling the sun and breeze, maybe even getting sweaty and dirty, is as much a pleasure if not more so, than eating the ripe tomatoes or bringing a freshly cut bouquet into the house. If you love gardening (or anything that you do that engages your soul), you lose track of time and are absorbed in the present moment. That very quality distinguishes that which feeds you or gives you energy from that which depletes you. One person's onerous task is another person's joy.

A green-thumb teacher, therapist, editor, mentor, director, mother, or vision carrier for the potential in another is like a gardener who loves what she does, knowing what is fragile and tentative and needs to be treated tenderly, what is valuable and meaningful, and what requires pruning-shears discrimination. People grow and bloom with you when such is the case. And you, in turn, are also affected by the degree to which you are challenged to grow yourself.

As women enter into the crone years, involvement in such work will change. Children become independent adults, retirement arrives or is on the horizon, moving on becomes an option or a necessity, predictable and unpredictable events happen. It's not only that outer circumstances change; your thoughts, feelings, and dreams may also shift and change. Many women now feel a pull toward solitude for reflection, self-expression, inner development, or just plain time off from others. Inner time is especially needed at the beginning of a new season of your life. A crone takes stock and decides how large a garden and what will be in it, in her season to come.

Women have always had to juggle many roles. This was true when women were mostly full-time wives and mothers, and now when women also have work or careers, it is more true than ever. Women's lives always called for flexibility and coping skills, but the traditional life itself was much more predictable. The generation of women who created the Women's Movement or were beneficiaries of the opportunities that came from it traveled down new paths. There weren't many footsteps to follow, or much in the way of foremothers. We became role models, cheering sections, sounding boards, and green-thumb support for each other. Being a woman with longtime good friends is like taking an experiential group seminar in surviving change. We learned through the stories our friends were living and lived our own experiment at the same time. Now we watch ourselves growing older.

In the prime crone years, many wise women who love their work decide to work less, be selective about what they will do, or focus on major creative undertakings. For others, full retirement can be liberating. Finally, there is time for yourself, for your own pursuits, creativity, pastimes and interests. Working women who had to put in forty-hour weeks, commute, and maintain households may have had very little disposable time or income, and yet, if you are now a crone, you nonetheless kept your own small garden, cultivating interests, and collecting seeds of possibilities to plant, and now *finally* there is time for them and for you.

Gardening requires vigilance. There are small pests and large destructive ones that need to be fenced out. I live where families of deer view gardens as restaurants, for example. For metaphoric gardens, the threat is usually the two-legged variety. As women who work at home have long realized, unless you build strong boundaries around your own time, other people assume that they can intrude with their needs. Once you retire, boundary-keeping skills are absolutely necessary. The garden that is *you* is the one that most needs a green thumb and strong fences.

4

CRONES TRUST WHAT THEY KNOW IN THEIR BONES

CRONES TRUST their instincts about people and principles. This trust grows through growing older and wiser, through learning from life. A painful lesson taken to heart makes an impression. A crone can ruefully laugh at Isabel Allende's apt observation, attributed to a grandmother in her novel, *City of the Beasts:* "Experience was what you learned just after you needed it." (Amen to that!)

Looking back on lessons learned, many women realize that they were relatively clueless about potentially dangerous situations, or had been impulsive and heedless. Some realize that they disregarded an uneasy feeling or even a stab of fear, and rather than appear impolite, foolish, snobbish, prejudiced, selfish, or ignorant, became a victim instead. A bad experience provides a dose of wisdom for a woman who becomes a crone: it is another victimization for a woman who does not become wiser from the experience.

As we age, having trustworthy instincts about who to trust and who to be wary of becomes especially important. Larcenous people prey on older women with misleading mailings and solicitous phone scams. "Trust me" insincerity is everywhere. Fortunately, trusting one's own instincts improves with practice. A woman who heeds the inner crone can be politely rude, saying "No, thank you," without listening further, and hang up on a caller. She can change doctors or lawyers or seek a second opinion when something feels "off" about a consultation. She doesn't hire someone, nor does she keep someone in her employ when she feels a sense of unease or recognizes bad character. She pays attention to a feeling that there is a danger in remaining where she is, or a recognition that something is wrong when she knows that her feelings are being manipulated. A wise woman knows herself and has learned from experience to heed such messages from herself. She knows the difference between encountering a warning signal and having a cautionary nature.

Women's intuition has been much maligned. It's a wisdom having to do with living things, plants, animals, people, illness, birth, and death. It's also a receptivity to energy and other invisible realms. An ordinary woman attending to a dying person draws upon crone wisdom when she instinctively or intuitively knows what to do. This parallels how many new mothers are maternally wise, something common enough to be unremarkable until a young mother refuses to follow the advice of an authority, sensing in her heart and mind that this would be wrong for her particular child.

Credentials and recommendations are taken into account, after which a crone will make decisions about who to trust to look after her, her health, and her assets, based on her sense of caregivers' and managers' competency, character, and compassion, and on something that "feels right" between them. This is a soul connection, or (in the philosopher Martin Buber's words) an *I-Thou* relationship, which is a deep in-the-bones knowledge of mutuality when two souls meet.

I chose the title "Close to the Bone" when I wrote a book about life-threatening illnesses, because I knew that the prospect of death can bring patients and those who love them close to the bone—or to the soul. Sometimes it takes a life-threatening illness for folks to pay attention to this, and sometimes it's only in the last months or years of a person's life that the soul shines and is seen through the transparency of an ailing body.

The absence of words for something handicaps its development, as does the denigration of words associated with women. It may help to learn some Greek: the Greeks have two words for knowledge: *logos* and *gnosis*. What can be learned through education and scientific inquiry is *logos*. What can be known through intuitive feelings and spiritual or mystical experiences is *gnosis* (no-sis). Logos is rational, objective, logical, expressible in words or numbers, while gnosis is subjective, non-rational, nonverbal, feeling-tinged, expressible through poetry, images, metaphor, and music, and is often unproveable by its very nature. Every sacred experience is subjective: the sense of oneness with the universe, or with divinity, a spiritual epiphany, a timeless moment infused with beauty, spiritual insight, and grace is gnosis. Ineffable yet profoundly transformative—these are soul experiences. Crones trust what they know in their bones from experiences such as these.

5

CRONES MEDITATE IN THEIR FASHION

LONG BEFORE the gurus came to America with mantras and meditation, women in training to be crones as well as crones themselves found time and ways to meditate. It may have been called "washing the dishes and staring out the window," or "folding laundry and thinking," or "daydreaming," or "doing nothing." It may have begun as having a quiet cup of tea or coffee before the household awoke with its hullabaloo of getting everyone out the door. It may have been what you did while taking a walk, or even what you did in commuter traffic. It was a time when a thought could come to mind, or something beautiful truly seen, or a dream or conversation remembered. It was like an open-ended Quaker kind of internal meeting, in which silence invited thoughts, images, and feelings to be brought into a spacious place in your mind or heart, observed, wondered about, or pondered over lightly.

Women who worry incessantly are *not* meditating. Going over "she said, he said" conversations or having worst-case thoughts is not meditating. Meditation is not worry, nor is it preoccupation with past pain and resentments, nor is it making up to-do lists. Focus, in such cases, may be inward, but there is no open space for thoughts and connections to come to mind, or for feelings and images to rise to the surface and be observed without being attached to worry, guilt, or anger. Mindfulness is now taught, but it is naturally done by many women. If you like your own company, value time alone, and find as you grow older that you seem to have grown more introverted, chances are that you have been practicing your own form of meditation.

Maybe heartfulness more accurately describes what crones do. To hold something in your heart and ponder upon it is meditation. To hold someone in your heart without possessiveness, is also. As we grow older, the list of people who have died that we remember grows longer. In meditative moments, we can hold them tenderly in our hearts—in that place in the center of our chest, where we instinctively place our hands, one over the other, as a gesture that says, "I feel for you" or "I love you." Heartfulness and meditation come together in the instant we really see and appreciate something beautiful, and in this moment send the equivalent of a prayer as a postcard thank-you, as we let the beauty in.

To have quiet moments in daily life has gotten increasingly difficult, even in the third phase of life. Many crones make time for meditation as a spiritual practice, or as a means of stress reduction and time away from household and workplace in order to be alone with a roomful of others who leave them to meditate.

Inner life was meant to grow in importance as we grow older. We explore the world with our senses in earlier years, which are directed outward toward what we can see, hear, touch, smell, or taste, all of which usually become less acute as the years pass. As we grow older, we can draw from what we have already experienced. Usually we have more time for an inner life. Sleeping less than we used to gives us extra hours.

Understanding comes when we take time to notice patterns and can see events in a more detached way than when we were in the midst of them. Through such insight, our store of wisdom grows. When we take time for moments of reflection, we see the importance of character rather than surface appearance and realize that when people do what they do, it is more about them than it is about us.

Experience is the teacher in our early years. Stored as bits of memory, it becomes an inner resource, a personal collection of intangible memorabilia that we see from a different perspective later in life, especially in moments of reflection, when we find ourselves musing about past events and people in our hearts. When we do this, we see past relationships, ideas, and events in the light of a wiser consciousness. From the soul's standpoint, those quiet moments—when we are "doing nothing" or meditating in our fashion—are when creative thoughts and meaningful feelings and intuitions arise.

6

CRONES ARE FIERCE ABOUT
WHAT MATTERS TO THEM

GLORIA STEINEM has often noted that women tend to be more conservative when young, and become rebellious and radical as they grow older, while it's the opposite for men. Women become fiercely compassionate crones when they are outraged at the suffering caused as much by indifference by those in authority as by the perpetrators. Compassion and anger come together for terrorized, abused, helpless, and neglected people, whose plight is considered of little importance because they have no power or value in a world where greed and power over others rather than concern for others is the ruling principle. Crones are not naive or in denial about reality. When something in particular is an outrage, and doing something about it is a choice, a moment of truth occurs in which activists are born. The suffering of others or the feeling of *Enough is enough!* radicalizes older women.

Women become radicalized through empathy. It is not difficult for women to imagine and feel what it would be like to be helpless and abused, made worse by the indifference of those who could make a difference. Reality rather than imagination may be the source of empathy, when one in three women in the world will have been beaten or raped in their lifetime and everyday violence requires that women always be alert to this possibility.

A crone is a woman who has found her voice. She knows that silence is consent. This is a quality that makes older women feared. It is not the innocent voice of a child who says, "the emperor has no clothes," but the fierce truthfulness of the crone that is the voice of reality. Both the innocent child and the crone are see-ing through the illusions, denials, or "spin" to the truth. But the crone knows about the deception and its conse-quences, and it angers her. Her fierceness springs from the heart, gives her courage, makes her a force to be reckoned with.

The fierce compassion of a crone is an outgrowth of mother-bear maternal protectiveness felt for those be-yond her immediate nuclear family. Among indigenous peoples, "grandmother" is a title of respect for an old-er woman in a society that had councils of wisewomen elders, women beyond childbearing years whose own children were grown, and whose maternal concern was now for all the children of the tribe and for generations to come. A mother bear is fiercely protective of her young; what is less well-known is that she also practices a form of "tough love" when her grown cubs are able to take care of themselves but would rather she contin-ue to provide for them. She runs them up a tree with her fierceness. When they finally decide to come down, they are on their own, and if they are to eat and survive they must use the skills she taught them.

It is the exceptional power of the mother bear coupled with her maternal concern that demands respect and fear. Smaller creatures, including human mothers, are also fiercely maternal, but they are often not powerful enough to be feared or strong enough to protect their offspring. While brute force still has to be reckoned with in some human situations, civilization measures power economically and politically. In the Western world, women have been acquiring power through education and positions of authority, and men are learning that it is a mistake to underestimate a woman's passion for social justice and power to expose wrongdoing.

Wrongdoing that provokes mother-bear fierceness is almost always both a betrayal of trust and an exploitation of others. This is compounded if a woman is discounted or treated punitively when she initially brings information to light. This further betrayal fuels determination and fierceness, rather than shuts her up as intended.

7

Crones Choose the
Path with Heart

CRONES ARE WOMEN who learn from experience
and can apply past lessons to present choices. Seeing
the consequences of their actions teaches them lessons
they take to heart. They are women who are passion-
ate, courageous, or principled, yet were once heedless of
the harm they could cause by acting on impulse. As one
woman ruefully said, "I used to let the chips fall where
they may."

Fear of being a wimp or the romance of being swept
away ruled the day, or a cautionary warning was taken

47

as a challenge or dare. Only later would they see how they and innocent others suffered because of this. Major consequences might have been averted, if only women had gone about decision-making more slowly and thoughtfully. Lessons were also learned by women who gave in and gave up on what was important to them in the past, and as crones, resist being manipulated or bullied to do what someone else wants.

Crones know when they are at a fork in the road and understand that the decision to be made will cost whatever the alternative is. Choosing one path means giving up the other. Every major decision has its own specifics and particulars: the details differ, but one essential remains the same. You must know yourself and what matters to you in order to choose wisely.

Following a path with heart, staying juicy, and being content are related. I have paraphrased Don Juan's teachings to his apprentice Carlos Castaneda ever since I read them in the 1960s. My version: There are many paths to choose from, and none of them go anywhere. Yet you must carefully choose which path you will take.

If you choose a path with heart, it may be difficult, but there is joy along this path, and as you travel, you grow and become one with it. If you choose a path out of fear, anxiety travels with you, and no matter how much power, prestige, and possessions you acquire, you will be diminished by it. The adage is true: it is the journey, not the destination that matters.

The thought that we are spiritual beings on a human path, rather than human beings who may or may not be on a spiritual path, has intrigued me since it first entered my mind. If we have an immortal soul and if life has a purpose, why might we be here? Might each of us need to find a personal answer to the question, *What did we come to do?*

Might love be at the heart of every question that has to do with the meaning of a particular life or of a special moment? To be human is to love and then be vulnerable to loss and suffering. Might the suffering we experience and the suffering we cause be a means for us to learn? Might healing and forgiving be part of this path? Might trust and courage develop only when we risk loss? Might compassion grow through shared human experiences? Might how we react to what we cannot prevent be part of this curriculum? Might two other questions then be, *What did we come to learn?* and *Who or what did we come to love?*

These are questions that we hope to answer well by the end of life. These are also questions that can be asked about every significant relationship or commitment. (What did I come to do, to learn, to love, or to heal?) They are questions that only the person whose life it is can really answer.

To be human is a body and soul experience, unique for each person. On a physical level, no one is the same as anyone else. Each of us has our own unique story, the fulfillment of which has to do with choosing the path with heart. We come into the world with a particular disposition: the way we innately are can be seen in infancy. The predispositions we unpack along the way in response to what we encounter. What talents did we come with? What do we find fascinating? What gives us joy? What do we know matters deeply to us? If we are spiritual beings on a human path, the answers to the questions that shape the journey do not come from outside of us, for the wisdom that knows is within us.

The outer path we take is public knowledge, but the path with heart is an inner one. The two come together when who we are that is seen in the world coincides with who we deeply are. As we grow wiser, we become aware that the important forks in the road are usually not about choices that will show up on any public record; they are decisions and struggles to do with choosing love or fear; anger or forgiveness; pride or humility. They are soul–shaping choices.

In ancient Greece, at important junctures or major forks in the road, the traveler could find a statue of Hecate, goddess of the crossroads, a curious image with three faces, which symbolized her ability to see three directions at once. She could see the path that had brought you here, and looked down the two roads that you might take. She was a crone, whose symbol was also the waning moon. She is also an image of that wise part of ourselves which has learned from experience and observation, listens to what we intuitively know, and takes reality, ourselves, and the well-being of others into consideration before she acts. A woman who has grown wiser as well as older is aware of being at an important fork in the road. It may be a moment of truth: whatever she says will have an impact, and once said cannot be taken back. It may be a moment of choice: she is voting with her feet or putting her body on the line, and something will never be the same afterward. It may be an intention that she means to keep: to let go of the past and forgive.

If you find yourself at such a crossroad, may you know which path has heart and have the courage to take it.

8

CRONES SPEAK THE TRUTH
WITH COMPASSION

MOST WOMEN become adept at supportive conversations, a practice that lends itself to becoming superficial, when uncomfortable truth or differences of opinion habitually don't pass through polite lips. Saying what others want to hear, rather than what is true, can become second nature. The challenge, which leads to becoming a crone, is learning how to be both truthful and compassionate. Observation is the first step: really listen to what is being said. Is this a conversation that you want to take deeper? Are you being polite or cowardly? Is there a point to saying something now? The wisdom of the inner crone is knowing when to speak and what to say.

Truth is sharp-edged: it is an instrument that can cause pain, wound, disfigure, or maim. Or, it can be a surgeon's scalpel that removes a malignancy or reconstructs a damaged face, and restores health or self-esteem.

Women are most inclined to withhold the truth from those emotionally most important to them, and in so doing nurture and sustain their weaknesses. If you are in an abusive relationship, you not only allow yourself to be oppressed by the worst in the other person, you are sustaining it. The crone within a woman knows this. Listen to her, and decide not to collaborate with this abuse. Especially if it is coming from a son or daughter, and this bad behavior has been rationalized by bad psychology. The crone knows when something is wrong that needs to be faced. If you listen to the inner crone, a principle to remember is that *Doing is becoming*: by enacting crone behavior, you grow into being a courageous and wise woman.

To not want to embarrass a friend and withhold the truth does not serve her: friends tell each other the truth. Bad breath? Inattentive to appearance? Concern about use of alcohol? These could be signs of depression brought on by loneliness or loss, could be symptoms of medical, metabolic, or nutritional problems, could be side-effects from a prescribed medication or alcohol used to self-medicate or preoccupation with an unshared worry. Maybe your spouse's or friend's mind is slipping and even if this were the case, to do or say nothing withholds information when the timing could be crucial. A crone wants to know what the truth is—to help herself and those she loves. This may mean she will take herself or accompany a friend to an appointment with a doctor, a lawyer, or an AA meeting.

Crones value themselves and their relationships: who matters to you and to whom do you really matter? Among your acquaintances and friends, are there people who drain you and whose sense of entitlement, persistent invitations, or neediness manipulates you into spending time with them? I think about the women with cancer whose stories I drew from when I wrote *Close to the Bone*, who told me that "cancer was the cure for their codependency," meaning that they finally felt that they had a good enough excuse to not see people who made them feel guilty if they didn't listen to them or spend time with them. Like cancer patients, wise crones know that their time and energy are precious: *Whatever you do takes from what you otherwise could have done.*

If the truth is that it is time to end some relationships in order to have time for yourself and for those people in your life who really matter, this truth needs to be faced and the intention to do so has to be acted upon. To be truthful and kind are principles, how to do so and if it can be done, is the challenge.

The easiest to pare down are the reciprocal, social back-and-forths. Here, all that you may need to do is fade away. Holiday greeting-card acquaintances fit in this category. All it may take is two consecutive years of not hearing from you. Same principle applies to making social excuses to invitations. The message sent by not being available is an ambiguous one, open to interpretation. When fading away works, there is no tension at crossing paths at mutually attended functions later.

The most draining and difficult relationships never seem to end this easily, and these are a real challenge. It is hard to hold the intention if confronted: whatever you say may be defensive and lead to "caving in" and continuing as before. Or it can ensnare you in a round of guilt-and-blame conversations that can only do harm. It helps to remember Br'er Rabbit's efforts to get away from Tar Baby if you are tempted to blame the other person for your wish to get away from him or her.

Better to attribute your withdrawal to some changes going on in yourself. It could be due to introversion, a need for solitude for your creativity, a commitment that takes all your time, accompanied by the request that this effort be respected. A woman with a cancer diagnosis said she told several such people to no longer expect that she would be available for phone conversations and visits, because, as she told them, "I need all the energy I have to heal."

The decisiveness and clarity of a message that something is over is a kindness if the alternative to reach the same end is a long, drawn-out, painful process. Especially when unreciprocated romantic feelings are involved. Juicy crones are attractive people, who may be divorced or widowed and interested or not in finding a new partner. Selective dating services and Internet match-making websites have become a mainstream method of meeting potentially eligible men. Unintentional meetings happen, especially when women go places on their own. Meetings occur in the time-honored way in which unmarried people meet each other—friends make introductions. As a result, men whose attentions are not welcomed can turn up in your life and become enamored and persistent, failing to get or heed the message that you are not interested. A crone ends such relationships cleanly, clearly, and respectfully. She does not feel guilt or blame for his unreciprocated feelings. She knows she did not lead him on or owe him anything, even if he feels differently and says so. What she is unambivalently clear about is that it is over.

If you are a woman who can't act decisively, you will give in if he persists and go out with him, or will feel sorry for him and see him again, or tell him not to call and then engage in long conversations when he does. You may think that it would be mean, or at least not nice, to do otherwise. I have an image for you, if such is the case, that might help you to be firm and decisive. Think about the practice of bobbing the tails of cocker spaniel puppies: it would not be kind to cut the tail off an inch at a time, especially when the task can be done with one clean, sharp, and decisive severing.

The Healing and
Liberating Power of Truth

Many crones know that truth liberates. It takes courage to be self-revealing, when "don't tell anyone" or "what will the neighbors think?" were drummed into you in childhood. Many women need to feel compassion for the traumatized or shamed child they still harbor in themselves, as well as breaking the hold that shame has on them. When such is the case, truth is blocked and an emotional wound remains unhealed.

Crones don't live under false pretenses or cower in fear of being condemned or rejected, shrinking back at significant moments from uncomfortable conversations. To feel ashamed is to be doubly oppressed: first by whatever it was, and then by the sense of unworthiness because of it. Many women have been abused as children, or come from uneducated, alcoholic, or impoverished families, or have had abortions, or are closeted lesbians, or grew up keeping family secrets. At some point in their lives, most remember fearing that this truth would become known. Crones, however, also recall when and with whom they broke this taboo of silence as the beginning of feeling whole. To speak the truth is to be able to say, this is who I am.

It's never just what happened, but always how you respond to what happened, that matters. Hidden as a secret, you are a victim, alone with your suffering. When you find the courage to speak the truth, you begin to liberate yourself from the past that otherwise holds you hostage.

Crones are in the habit of speaking the truth.

9

CRONES LISTEN TO THEIR BODIES

WE USUALLY DO pay attention to our outer appearance, typically noticing whatever part of our bodies we are unhappy about. It behooves us, however, to get on very good terms with more than just the surface of our bodies as we grow older; for if we don't listen to our bodies and pay attention to our physical needs and pleasures, this vehicle that we need to be running well to take us into a long and comfortable life, will instead limit what we can do and who we become. Besides, if we listen to our bodies, they often teach us to pay attention to something important that we might otherwise miss or ignore.

A crone learns that fulfilling what both body and psyche desire brings about a sense of well-being; for example, when women who want to dance make time for it. If dancing is a joy, then endorphins are released, enhancing pleasure and diminishing aches and pains. Welcomed touch is something else that nurtures body and psyche and makes us feel like purring. Bodies like orgasms, too. A dance class, a regular massage, pets, a vibrator are within reach of a crone; so no whining about not having a husband who dances, or a lover! Some bodies yearn to be touched by the sun. Others want to feel the wind or the crisp mountain air. Some bodies are energized by travel or walking for miles. A crone listens to her body as an extension of her psyche. When the two are together about what matters or what is desired, then images, emotions, and memories are intertwined with physical sensations and activities. Psyche and body are as one.

Many crones also learn to listen to their bodies in the same way that some people are attuned to the vibrations and sounds of their automobiles, and can tell when something is "off," and what might need attending to. This is about bothering to pay attention, which for many comes only after something goes wrong. For others, the listening is second nature.

Our bodies also often express feelings for us, and if we do not allow emotions to surface as our feelings, they can come out as our pain or a physical symptom. Unshed tears of grief, an anniversary reaction—the body remembers emotion-laden dates when the mind has forgotten. Unacknowledged anger, resentment, or hostility, or tension from fear or anxiety may come out as an ache or a pain, as an asthmatic wheeze, or a bowel disorder, insomnia, or show up as a rash. A crone listens for the underlying message between her feelings and her body. It makes her seek an inner answer to "What is the matter?" when a familiar physical symptom arises.

A crone also pays attention to her body's perceptions—she listens to what it is saying about people and situations. Who do you draw physically close to? Who do you step back from when they come close? Goose-bumps, tightening jaw muscles, blushing, feeling the hair on the back of your neck stand up, are especially important messages to interpret. Whenever they arise, your body is telling you something.

What a crone looks like on the surface may or may not matter to her. What does matter is that her worth as a woman and a human being are not dependent on this. After menopause, the effects of gravity usually become more evident. Everything tends to sag and be less firm. Such things as the healthy glow of someone who is physically fit and in good health, a twinkle in the eye, a genuine smile, and spontaneous laughter all go into making a person attractive regardless of age. However, crones who want to look as young as they feel sometimes will do something about their wrinkles and sags, while others love their wrinkles, graying or white hair, and enjoy looking grandmotherly or like a wise elder.

10

CRONES IMPROVISE

MOST CRONES could define their lives as an improvised work in process. Wherever they are at this moment in their lives was not a planned destination. It could be said that they have had many "incarnations" in this life, looking back upon many phases, places, and people who were important at different stages in their lives. The singer and actress Madonna may be celebrated as a role model for reinventing herself, but such is in fact the case for many women, especially those around sixty, who grew up through wars and major social revolutions which affected them personally. There has been no single track for us to be on.

It's not at all unusual for this generation to have married more than once, have had live-in relationships and several or many sexual partners. Some had children early and are grandmothers. Some became mothers late as others their same age were entering early menopause. Some remarried and raised blended families. Some adopted orphans from foreign countries.

As a crone-aged woman, your family of origin may be geographically far away from where you live now. You may also be living a far different life from theirs. Depending on marital status and circumstance, you could have lived in poverty or on welfare, managed as an unemployed single parent, married wealth, or been a suburban mom—at different times in your life. You may have begun your own business, or made and lost paper profits in stocks. You or women you know may live or have lived in a commune or an ashram, be part of a Buddhist sangha, or become a Protestant minister.

You could have entered professions and occupations which once did not allow women into them or admitted only token women, or you may have been a full-time homemaker, or been employed in a traditional woman's job. You may even have stayed in the same town, married to the same man, and raised a family.

Regardless of what came before, changes in circumstance usually happen during the crone years. Retirement begins, which can last longer than your active work life if you take early retirement and have a long lifespan. Women usually outlive their husbands, making widowhood a whole new phase. Nests empty, and the fledglings may end up living far away.

Flexibility, resourcefulness, good health, friends, the ability to learn and keep on growing, being needed or doing service, having absorbing interests, and the ability to enjoy your own company, are qualities and possibilities that make improvising a good life possible. With curiosity and an adventuresome spirit, some crones discover a whole new world of interest. Some finally take something up that has lain fallow for decades. There are late-bloomers in all aspects of life. When Mom becomes a widow, for example, her grown children often are surprised at how independent she becomes, how much she travels or takes care of the business.

The crone phase is a time when many women look for ways to "give back." Well aware of how many opportunities they had, crones fill volunteer ranks in every community, are advocates and activists at every level.

A crone is herself. She accepts change, appreciates the good in her life, grieves for what dies or loses vitality, and goes on. Her identity is not defined by her social or occupational roles; what she does and who she shares her life with are expressions of who she is, not her identity. When it's time to let go of one phase of her life, she can, which makes a next phase possible. Truth is, she does not exactly reinvent herself intentionally; rather she is improvising, adapting to change, responding to what engages her energy. If the metaphor is music, her instrument is herself and the deep theme of her song follows the beat of her heart. Each phase is like a different movement in a major work, with variations on her theme. Until the music ends, crones will improvise.

11

CRONES DON'T GROVEL

THERE WAS THE INSTANT recognition of *I know exactly what you mean* laughter, when one juicy crone in a circle of women said, "I don't grovel for approval anymore." Truly, a *that was then, this is now* comment about a compelling need to please a man that those who laughed ruefully recognized. Not that anyone in the room was admitting to having actually groveled, but each knew the feeling—the anxious effort to please and be pleasing, and the silent questions that went with it. "Am I good enough or pretty enough?" "Do I please you?"

71

How sad and how pathetic we were in the awful years of feeling awkward, rejectable, and therefore relieved to be acceptable. Decades have passed since high school, and yet many women have vivid memories of the time when being popular really mattered. Mean and thoughtless words said then still can carry a sting. When wearing clothes with the right labels counted, and who you were seen with mattered more, out-of-style or not-good-enough friends found themselves shed as new cliques formed. This was especially so when there were clubs or sororities. Groveling to be acceptable to a popular group of girls was a sure way of becoming humiliated. Adolescent insecurity doesn't foster compassion; instead it fosters an attitude of superiority through putting others down.

I think the conversation about groveling could have gone further and deeper, if it could have become more serious, opening to talk about how it was to be the ones with the power to reject, and how this made us feel at the time and now. Women as well as men identify with the oppressor and do to others what was done to them.

Seeing this in yourself is an uncomfortable insight, but when acknowledged and accompanied by regret and remorse, it's definitely a learning experience.

Women entering their crone years often revisit feelings they had in high school because menopause has similarities with adolescence. It is a hormonal and physiological period of transition and uncertainty, when insecurity about attractiveness once again rears its head. Young women *and* menopausal women feel too fat or too flat, or too much or not enough. Older women do feel themselves becoming invisible, especially if attractiveness is part of their personal magnetism.

Wanting to please is normal. However, being willing to grovel goes way beyond wanting to please. Think of the difference in demeanor between a beaten dog who cringes and wags her tail at the same time, versus a healthy puppy who wiggles with delight and is eager to please. Nature has made the young of all species vulnerable and cute, appealing to the protective and nurturing qualities in adults. We all come into the world to be loved, which is an essential ingredient needed for growth of the body and psyche. If we are loved, accepted, and treated well, we don't grovel; we act naturally and spontaneously.

When groveling occurs between two adults, fear of punishment (which can be rejection) exists. It is a hierarchical relationship in which one person has power over the other and is exercising it. Groveling is a psychological state of mind in which you defer to another person because you think of yourself as a needy, unworthy inferior. Groveling can also result from being in an abusive relationship that you don't leave when you could. Only a woman who is actually a prisoner or has the legal status of property has to grovel. All others need to get help and get out.

Inequality that is built in as a part of culture fosters low self-esteem. Feminism made women aware that this is a fundamental assumption of patriarchy. Whenever men or white people assume they are automatically superior and entitled to deference, women and minorities suffer from being treated as inferiors. Inequality leads to abuse of power by those in power, which harms them at a soul level as well as hurts those they oppress.

There are lots of women who are nongroveling crones today because of feminism. Equality as a principle, reproductive choice, the availability of opportunities and support to become an authentic and whole person cannot be taken for granted, when none of these were in the culture prior to the Women's Movement. While crones agree that "Nobody can make you feel inferior without your consent," a saying attributed to Eleanor Roosevelt (who became a crone without the movement), I think that without the Women's Movement, only an exceptional woman could become a crone.

12

CRONES LAUGH TOGETHER

THE BELLY LAUGHTER of women together is something that usually happens in the absence of men. It's a
spontaneous potluck of sharing that often arises in the
midst of talk that is very real and true. Laughter arises
in response to tales told on one's self that are "could have
been me" stories of embarrassing or triumphant past
moments. The stories and laughter builds and bubbles,
and a general state of hilarity results. It's never the same
retold, it's a "you had to be there" laughter. It's laughter in which endorphins, the healing, well-being mol-
ecules of emotion flow. Crones together are most likely

to laugh until tears flow because they know when they are with like-hearted women and don't need to preserve a persona. There's no pecking order here.

When I have explained women's healing laughter to mixed audiences, I have commented that crones will report afterward, "I laughed so much, I could have wet my pants," and then I pause and say, "and being post-menopausal, . . ." which is invariably followed by a wave of laughter from the women in the audience, those who very well know that this actually happens. This is a glimpse of healing humor, which acknowledges and makes light of difficulties that unite rather than divide us. It's a slice of shared life.

Men have accused women of having no sense of hu-mor because we don't laugh at jokes that men think of as funny. Freud's analysis of humor as being hostile helps explain why we might not (especially when directed at women). Then there are jokes that little boys tell that is scatological or toilet humor, which grown men still find funny. Little girls and grown women don't get why.

Difficulties between the sexes have made some women describe the challenge as being an "interspecies communication" problem. This seems to apply especially to humor. However, humor as an outlet for hostility or superiority has an appeal to both sexes. Dumb blonde jokes, mother-in-law jokes, put-down humor in general, including male-bashing jokes, are all outlets for hostility. This kind of humor does not leave people with a sense of well-being, and the quality of laughter is different. Compared to hilarity or healing laughter, there is an absence of affection.

The comfort level which invites laughter among women comes from a sense of being among one's own; however deeply one loves specific men, men often do feel like a separate species. As Carolyn Heilbrun, in *The Last Gift of Time,* mused: "Doris Lessing has wondered if anyone observing humankind might not conclude that men and women were different species, so diverse are their habits, obsessions, and pastimes. It is an idea that has occurred to all women at one time or another." This sense of being among one's own is not a universal feeling among women, it depends upon the shared archetypal sense of sisterhood.

The laughter of crones comes from a deep well of feeling. It's an expression of the triumph of spirit and soul over that which could have broken us or made us bitter; it's because whatever happened or didn't happen didn't turn us into whiners. Sometimes it comes close to gallows humor; that regardless of how old we are or what shape we may be in, at this moment we are still here and are laughing together. Hilarity is a spontaneous expression of freedom and celebration.

13

CRONES SAVOR THE GOOD
IN THEIR LIVES

IF YOU ARE A WOMAN who has enjoyed life and not become soured by your personal share of human suffering, you are likely to become a crone who is a connoisseur of experience—meaning that you are able to savor the good that comes your way. It's an appreciation of everyday grace. Crones know how fortunate they are to still be alive, when most of the world's people do not live beyond fifty and many of their friends didn't make it this far either.

Savoring is about giving an experience your full attention and truly taking it in. Savoring is about gratitude for this moment. If you are a crone with an eye for nature's beauty, you may see a gorgeous sunrise, or geese flying overhead in formation against a blue sky, or pick up a perfectly formed seashell on the beach, and in the "ahhhh" of visual appreciation, there's a "thank-you." Or you may hear a cello concert by YoYo Ma, and in the poet T.S. Eliot's words from *Four Quartets,* it was "music heard so deeply, that you are the music while the music lasts." Or you may savor a fine old cognac and be aware of the mellowness of both it and this moment.

While it is true that someone who had never seen the beauty of nature like this before, or heard YoYo Ma, or drunk a fine cognac could also savor any of these experiences, crones take in special moments in life knowing how special they truly are. This is further enhanced by awareness of how fleeting and precious life is, and by having an "attitude of gratitude," a phrase M. J. Ryan made into a book title.

Gratitude comes from being conscious of alternative possibilities and the big picture. Crones breathe a "thank-you," for example, when they could have hit the pedestrian they hadn't seen, or stopped just inches away from the car that suddenly braked in front of them. Crones are grateful for the report that the mammogram was fine, or of the uneventful delivery of a healthy new grandchild. Crones are grateful that their minds still work, or that their bodies do. Some mornings, crones wake up thankful to be alive. Crones have known bad times and bad days. Crones have also known magic moments and times when things could not be better. With an appreciation and an appetite for life, when things go well or something delicious happens, crones savor it.

Gratitude is something we have inside us that rises to the surface when something in particular invites it out. Gratitude is a wonderful spiritual practice, actually. Every time you breathe an "ahhhh" or savor a moment, a thank-you for being alive is rising from your soul to fill your heart. Yes, it's about the beauty of seeing the geese flying overhead, but it's more: it's a thank-you to the geese, to nature, to the creator. And even more than this, it's a thank-you that I am here, and that I have a place in the universe. Yes, it's about being at this particular concert, but it's more: it's gratitude that such music could be composed and played, and that I can hear it. And even more than this, it's gratitude for something beyond words, for the communion.

Just as a connoisseur of wine has to have discriminating taste buds, a lot of experience drinking wine, and acquired a great deal of knowledge about wine before be coming a connoisseur, the equivalent is true for anyone considered a connoisseur of anything. One usually starts with a love of whatever it is, first.

Crones are connoisseurs of life's good moments.

3

POSSIBILITIES AND THOUGHTS

1

EXCEPTIONAL MEN
CAN BE CRONES

WHEN I WAS ON A book tour for *Goddesses in Older Women*, there was, as expected, a preponderance of women in my audiences, but usually a handful of men attended, more so when the lectures were sponsored by Jungian groups. As I spoke positively about crone qualities to these audiences, I found myself saying, "Exceptional men can be crones," because it's true. I also began to think that it's high praise to say of a man, "he's a crone," just as it is a major compliment to call a woman a *mensch*, which is the Yiddish word for "man" when she courageously speaks up and takes a public position in the face of potential retribution.

I think of the men that I know who are crones. Most are men in the third phase of their lives with little investment in persona, who made a commitment to helping, caring for, and looking after people who have needed them. Then there are men who would not have become crones, except through suffering themselves. Achievement of goals, recognition, and the perks that go with success were acquired, and then came a turning point. Hubris, the overweening pride that goes before a fall, might have turned into humility. Or he might have been plunged into a period of suffering and self-reflection after a major loss or a health crisis, and made use of psychotherapy. Such men may continue to have visible roles in the world, but the impression that they are making on others or the trappings of success no longer motivate them. Loss, or the possibility of loss, suffering, and recovery, provide an opportunity for successful men to learn who and what really matters. If they acquire wisdom and compassion through humility and remorse, then unnoticed and unheralded, they may quietly and inwardly become crones.

A man's innate psychology combined with how he was treated by older males when he was a child and a young adult has a huge influence on the possibility of him becoming a crone later in life.

In families headed by authoritarian fathers, as in patriarchies of all kinds, power matters most. Vulnerability is seen as a weakness, and boys aspire to become bigger and stronger, so that they may dominate others and not be humiliated themselves. Boys are often hazed, belittled, and humiliated by older boys or bigger boys in the schoolyard, and in many households by their older siblings. The same pattern usually continues into adolescence and young adulthood. Fraternities perpetuate this in their initiations, and it is institutionalized in the military. The psychology of it boils down to "what was done to me, I will do to you when it is my turn to have the upper hand," and is justified by the notion that "this will make boys into men." Pleasure in inflicting emotional or physical pain on others is usually most enjoyed by boys or men who have been abused themselves. The lack of compassion shown them stunts this development, and identification with the oppressor rather than the victim is the norm when this is so.

Even in its most benign expression, the dominator-hierarchical alpha-male pattern begins very early and continues through adulthood. It becomes second nature for men to check out whether they are one-up or one-down as part of everyday life, especially if fear of a bigger and stronger male was instilled at home. This is a major social factor that makes development of crone qualities the exception rather than the rule in men.

In contrast, men who as boys and young men became protective big brothers of their younger siblings or who had fathers or older brothers who were affectionate and mentoring have an advantage.

Men who become involved in the childbirth process—going with their wives to prenatal classes and to the labor and delivery room—describe feeling an upwelling of awe and tenderness toward their newborn babies. This can be a profound bonding experience. These men usually become involved in caring for and playing with their infants and children and in doing so are developing nurturing, sustaining, and caretaking qualities (aspects of the feminine principle) in themselves. As nurturing men become valued and value this side of themselves, there will be more who become crones later in life. In older men, there is a natural lessening of aggression and ambition, which is physiologically related to a reduction in testosterone and adrenaline levels. More time also becomes available for relationships and an inner life, which will further encourage the crone development in these men.

When retirement is on the horizon, the exceptional man who can become a crone has already mentored younger people, looked after others, and has formed deep and lasting relationships. He has grown psychologically and spiritually through a combination of suffering and whatever he used to grow through the experience: therapy, meditation, spiritual direction, a combination of developing or having an inner life and a sense of connection with a source of meaning. He is motivated and sustained by love rather than power and can be called by the honored title of "crone."

2

CRONES TOGETHER CAN CHANGE THE WORLD

IT'S AN EXTRAORDINARY time to be an American woman in the third phase of life, especially if we are between our mid-fifties and mid-seventies. Never before in history has there been a generation of crone-aged women such as us. We were in our childbearing years when "the Pill" was available, and the Roe v. Wade decision gave us reproductive rights over our own bodies. Never before could the majority of women be sexually active and be able to choose whether or when to have children. The right to have equal pay for equal work, affirmative action to make up for prior discrimination, equality of access to education and work made huge inroads into formerly all-male institutions and occupations. We as a generation pushed doors open that had never allowed women through them. We as individuals could make personal choices about how and with whom we would live because we had the right to say "no." The religious and spiritual beliefs we held, where or whether we worshiped was also up to us. Never before in history have women had such rights and had them so naturally as to think of this as normal. We are also the beneficiaries of material abundance and medical advances and have a lifespan greater than any generation before us. We have a gender-advantage as well, outliving men at every age.

What an enormous influence crones could have now! If even one out of ten American women over fifty became involved in changing the world for the better, there could be almost five million crone activists in these ranks. We have wisdom to offer and priorities that would make a difference. Women know that once a community becomes a safe place for children and women, everyone is safe. We know that preventing children from being abused also prevents them from growing up and abusing others. We aren't surprised to know that fetal brains in pregnant women who live in terror or are starving develop differently, as do the brains of children who live under such circumstances. Our common sense tells us what researchers conclude: children are healthier and families smaller when women have reproductive choice, and that if all women had access to birth control, it would be a step toward reducing the overpopulation problem, which would in turn affect the ecological crisis stemming from depletion of resources, and so on.

Women respond to stress differently than men do, which gives us a psychological and physiological advantage in working toward a peaceful resolution of conflict, especially in areas of age-old conflict and retribution. Men respond to stress with a "flight or fight" physiology: adrenaline increases, enhanced by testosterone. Women have a "tend and befriend" physiological response; oxytocin—the maternal bonding hormone—increases with stress, which is enhanced by estrogen. Women bond with each other and reduce stress through conversation, which gives us an advantage in peace talks. In contrast, alpha-male conflicts are about supremacy. If you put the leaders in the same room to negotiate peace, their conflict moves to a bargaining table. When the point is to win, compromising is either a weakness or a strategy. Defeat is a humiliation with plans of retribution solace for the loser, who fosters hatred into the next generation. Regardless of who wins, we know that women and children always lose. Maternal wisewomen must become involved in peace processes in sufficient numbers to change the pattern. In the absence of such women, crone wisdom has been so far represented by exceptional men who are crones, such as Nelson Mandela, Mahatma Gandhi, His Holiness the Dalai Lama, and Jimmy Carter.

Women's Circles

A grass-roots women's movement to bring peace to the world would begin with women meeting together in small groups. This is how the suffragettes began and how consciousness-raising groups became the Women's Movement. Through friendships, networking connections, and now the Internet, such a movement of women meeting together in circles, fostering growth of more circles, communicating ideas and suggestions for action, could grow geometrically and then exponentially, until there were a critical number of circles to be an influence on how humanity perceives and solves its problems. Behavior and attitudes change when a critical number of people adopt them. Victor Hugo's famous statement, "There is nothing so powerful as an idea whose time has come," describes the phenomenon.

I envision a third wave of grass-roots international feminism taking the form of women's circles with a spiritual center. When women come together and make a commitment to each other to be in a circle, especially one with a spiritual center, they are creating a vessel of transformation for themselves, and a vehicle for change in their world. The essential components are individual women who have the ability to form enduring and deep friendships with other women. It is not enough to be of the female gender, for many women do not trust other women but see them as competitors for men, or believe that women are inferior.

It is the sister, mother, and crone archetype in women that makes it possible for women to identify with each other across national, racial, and religious boundaries. It is the ability to feel an empathic connection that makes women able to imagine what it would be like to be on either side of the Israeli-Palestinian divide, or to be a woman under the Taliban, or a welfare mother in the United States. It is a point of view that doesn't see war as something to be won, but as a cause of death and suffering for everyone, especially innocent women and children. Mothers have always seen their eighteen to twenty year olds in uniforms as just their boys whose lives may end prematurely. Our generation has seen almost all of our previous enemies become allies or trade partners, which is no compensation for the personal loss. Walking through the Vietnam War Memorial, seeing name after name of young men and some young women, the futility and waste of war seeps into consciousness.

The invisible power of women's circles on the women in them grows out of the power that people have on one another, which is extraordinary. Anyone's self-esteem, accomplishment, development of talent, has to do with whether we have been listened to and valued, loved for ourselves, encouraged and supported to do what we believed we could do. When there is psychological or practical support for making a significant change, change is more likely to happen. That others believe in us, or have the same perspective we have, or are role models, has a powerful and invisible effect. The power to resist the collective comes from being in a small circle with like-minded others. It allows us to keep on in the face of ridicule or opposition that we don't know what we are talking about, or don't belong wherever it is that we want to be.

In 1999, I wrote *The Millionth Circle* about women's circles with a spiritual center and the potential they had to change the world, which led to the formation of an international millionth circle initiative. It was a visionary possibility combined with a how-to, which in its brevity and poetic quality, I thought of as a "Zen and the Art of

Circle Maintenance." The idea of "the millionth circle" was inspired by the success of the antinuclear war movement and the story of "the hundredth monkey," which sustained small groups of activists and encouraged them to keep on with their efforts in the face of collective disbelief that concerned citizens could stop the nuclear arms race between the United States and Soviet Russia.

"The millionth circle" is a metaphor; it is the circle that, added to those already formed, becomes a critical mass. It would bring the feminine principle of relatedness to the table (from households to nations) as an antidote to the effects caused by the ego and fear-driven needs of individual men to dominate others. The masculine principle, otherwise, is a goal focus that leads to personal achievement and striving for excellence, where competition furthers the development of individual talents and teamwork, fostering creativity, knowledge, science, and technology that can benefit others.

Of all the human beings, male and female, who have *ever* lived on planet Earth, we who are in the prime years of cronehood now were the first who, as a generation, have had the opportunity of being maternal women *and* achievers in the outer world. It has been possible for us to make choices and learn consequences, and integrate both feminine and masculine principles into our psyches. We could easily be a short-lived resource, a never-again historical fluke, if fundamentalist religions and the patriarchal attitude that they spawn have their way. Humanity is on a destructive course, one way or another, and life on this planet is endangered by male human beings with power. Time seems to be running out on *Homo sapiens*. Biologically, the continuation of the species has always been up to women. Now I think that it is up to crones—women and the exceptional men who deserve the name—to bring forth the *sapiens* (which means *wise* in Latin) in time to insure the spiritual, psychological, and intellectual continuation of humanity.

3

MUSINGS

ANGELES ARRIEN, anthropologist, author, and crone, left an indelible impression in my mind when I heard her speak of four guiding principles.

1. Show up.
2. Pay attention.
3. Speak your truth, and
4. Don't be attached to outcome.

Each stage of life contributes to learning what this really can mean. Paying attention, for example, extends to what is unsaid and implied, or even unconsciously signaled. Experience teaches that there can be painful consequences of speaking the truth, which is why it takes courage to speak truth to power or to an intimate. To learn the consequences of *not* speaking the truth is a whole other lesson in life that comes from remaining silent and having to live with oneself. Attachment to outcome is linked to our expectations: we have hopes or assumptions which lead to feeling disappointed or angry or surprised by the actual response. To not be attached to outcome is a spiritual position that paradoxically is often the most effective.

Over the years, I have spoken up, and because my nature and nurture did not make me fear-driven, it's easier for me than it would be for many people to speak the truth to power. It is also the nature of my work as a psychiatrist and Jungian analyst to bring difficult perceptions into consciousness. I have been a whistle-blower, and there were some unpleasant consequences, but there is no question in my mind or heart that it was worth doing. I have found that *Speak the truth* and *Do not be attached to outcome* are wise words—especially if you are speaking up about issues and taking a stand for a principle, or testifying. But when the concern is with people we love, we cannot *not* be attached to outcome. As crones, for example, we can see the problems that are likely to be encountered down the road that our grown children or grandchildren and others we love may take. With them in mind, I find myself amending the last precept by making a substitution: *Pray for best outcome.*

The precepts become:

1. Show up.
2. Pay attention.
3. Speak your truth, and
4. Pray for best outcome.

Life has taught me that I don't know what best outcome is for anyone, really. Tough times may lie ahead for someone we care deeply about if he or she continues in a particular direction, as we with our experience can see. But a change in direction will have unforeseen consequences as well. Either choice may lead to a make-or-break crisis. Knowing that each person has his or her own fate and destiny, particular lessons to learn, and personal myth to live out, and that we cannot control or even know the full potential of what lies ahead, I've come to the conclusion that in such circumstances *Speak your truth* and *Pray for best outcome* is the very best we can do.

I believe that prayer for best outcome has an effect; that it is like sending energy or angels or wisdom to be with the person we are praying for. I also have an intuition that *Pray for best outcome* in the place of *Don't be attached to outcome* is an expression of crone wisdom which is aligned with the maternal or feminine principle, expressed spiritually. It is about speaking your truth knowing that it is limited, and nurturing and sustaining those for whom you pray spiritually in whatever they do. It's about wanting and therefore being attached to whatever best outcome for them may be—with their whole lifetime and soul journey in mind.

I wonder what
is going to happen next?

I believe that every crone could come up with a saying or words that described something she has learned from her own experience (and that it would be good for you to muse upon this). I was reminded that one of my own was, *I wonder what is going to happen next?* by a friend who was setting off on an unpredictable trip with a group of people whose relationships with each other might be fraught. As she left, she said, "I'm going to take your mantra with me."

Years ago, in the midst of my own midlife transition, I had heard myself saying these words, because the only thing that seemed predictable was the unpredictability of each day's events. Since then, I have found them to be the best words and attitude to have when going through the choppy waters and storms that occur when people are going through times which change their lives and can change them. Anyone who thinks they are entitled to smoother sailing or better accommodations or different company, in the midst of the major transitions that we go through in this life, better disabuse themselves of any such ideas. Otherwise they will whine and not be prepared to grow and change.

I hope that I can "wonder what will happen next" when the last major transition from this life to whatever comes next happens to me. I also hope that the words on Sister Corita's poster will turn out to be true: ". . . that the rules will be fair and that there will be wonderful surprises." For the end of the crone phase is a mystery or veil that each of us will pierce through alone to something or nothing. I think of the three phases of the moon and the three phases of womanhood: waxing, full, and waning, and then note that the moon goes through one final phase in the cycle; the waning moon of the Crone becomes less and less distinct, until it disappears into the dark phase of the moon. This darkness is the final mystery that comes at the end of the crone phase of our lives.

As spiritual beings on a human path, what we do at a soul level in the third phase will likely turn out to be the most important. Wisdom, compassion, character, what we do with the life we were given, what we learned, and who we have become all matter. Knowing also, as even the scientific world attests, that we are part of an inter-connected universe, in which the smallest movement of a butterfly's wing could actually have an effect on the whole system, I can imagine that each of us generates ripples of influence through who we are, what we do, whether we love and if we pray, and that someday we shall know.

Love to you.

CRONES DON'T WHINE
RESOURCE GUIDE

The journey of aging is an adventure filled with wisdom, transformation, and empowerment. This comprehensive guide aims to assist you in stepping into the fullness of your crone years, offering a wealth of resources designed to enrich this significant phase of life. Within these pages, you'll find an array of tools from support groups and therapy options to self-help literature and online platforms, each carefully selected to inspire personal growth, health, and vitality.

This guide is your companion in navigating the rich landscape of aging, providing access to vibrant communities, holistic health practices, and creative expressions that resonate with the divine feminine within. It is designed to empower you with the wisdom and resources necessary to thrive during this stage of life.

We invite you to delve into the support groups, therapy options, and variety of educational materials compiled here, all specifically tailored to enhance your journey. Discover these offerings to grow, celebrate your inner strength, and fully embrace the vitality of your crone years. Allow this guide to support you as you continue to explore the depths of your being and the boundless opportunities for personal evolution and joy.

Support Groups and Communities

If you're on the lookout for online support groups and communities specifically tailored to the needs and interests of aging women, you're in luck. The digital age brings with it a plethora of vibrant options designed to cater to the unique challenges and opportunities faced by women as they navigate this empowering stage of life. These platforms offer more than just companionship; they provide a space for personal growth, mutual support, and the sharing of wisdom accrued over a lifetime.

Engaging with these communities can be a transformative experience, allowing you to connect with like-minded individuals who understand the nuances of aging. Whether you're seeking advice on navigating health changes, looking for tips on maintaining an active lifestyle, or simply in need of a space to share and celebrate life's triumphs and trials, these online groups offer a sanctuary.

SeniorNet.com, **The Third Age**, and **Seniorsite. com** are just a few examples of platforms that provide roundtable discussions, educational resources, and articles tailored to the needs and interests of senior women. These sites champion lifelong learning and social engagement, proving that personal growth knows no age limit.

For those who find joy in connecting over shared hobbies and interests, **Buzz50** and **Older Is Wiser** offer forums and blogs where you can engage in discussions ranging from literature and gardening to health and technology. Meanwhile, **GransNet** serves as a hub for grandparents seeking advice, camaraderie, and support on everything from childcare to personal wellness.

Never Mind the Bus Pass stands out for its humorous take on senior living, reminding us that age is but a number and that vitality and a zest for life persist well beyond retirement. This blend of humor, advice, and community support underscores the importance of maintaining a positive outlook and staying mentally and socially active as we age.

ElderChicks is a blog for senior women to share their stories, challenges, and triumphs, fostering a sense of community and mutual support.

While not exclusively for seniors, **Meetup** allows individuals to find and join local groups with shared interests, including groups specifically for seniors interested in activities like hiking, book clubs, and cultural outings.

These online support groups and communities are invaluable resources that not only offer support and guidance but also celebrate the richness and diversity of the aging experience. By participating in these platforms, you can tap into a wealth of knowledge, find solace in shared experiences, and forge meaningful connections that enrich your journey through the crone years.

Therapy Options

As you're navigating the complexities of aging, finding the right therapy and counseling options is crucial. Gerontological counseling and holistic therapies play a vital role in addressing the mental, emotional, and physical challenges that come with this stage of life. Here are some valuable resources where you can find specialized support:

Gerontological Counseling Resources

- **Psychology Today's Elders (65+) Therapist Directory:** An extensive directory that allows you to search for therapists specializing in elder care across the United States. This resource offers detailed profiles of mental health professionals, helping you to find someone who meets your specific needs.

- **The American Geriatrics Society:** Provides resources and support for healthcare professionals and patients alike, including a searchable directory for geriatric care. While it's more healthcare-oriented, it can be a starting point for finding specialists who understand the nuances of aging.

Types of Therapies and Where to Find Them

- **Cognitive Behavioral Therapy (CBT)** *and* **Acceptance and Commitment Therapy (ACT):** Both therapies are effective for a range of issues including anxiety, depression, and insomnia, which can be common in older adults. Websites like the **Association for Behavioral and Cognitive Therapies (ABCT)** provide directories to find qualified CBT and ACT therapists.

- **Geriatric Group Therapy and Reminiscence Therapy:** These can be found through local community centers, senior centers, or mental health clinics that offer group sessions specifically designed for older adults. Contacting local aging agencies or the **American Association for Geriatric Psychiatry** can provide leads to group therapies available in your area.

- **Occupational Therapy (OT): The American Occupational Therapy Association (AOTA)** offers a way to find occupational therapists who specialize in working with older adults, focusing on improving daily functional abilities.

Holistic and Alternative Therapies

- **MantraCare:** This platform offers insight into holistic approaches to geriatric counseling, emphasizing the importance of psychoeducation and supportive psychotherapy for older adults. MantraCare connects individuals with therapists who use comprehensive strategies to address mental health and well-being.

- **The National Center for Complementary and Integrative Health (NCCIH):** Provides information on alternative therapies such as mindfulness, meditation, and art therapy. While not a directory, it's a valuable resource for understanding how these practices can support mental health in older adults. Visit NCCIH.

It's vital to choose a therapist or counseling service that specializes in the unique needs of aging individuals, with consideration for the therapist's experience, the types of therapy offered, and alignment with your personal needs and goals. These resources can guide you in finding the right support to navigate the challenges and opportunities of aging with empowerment and grace.

Self-Help Books

Here are some widely recognized titles that align with the themes of aging, personal growth, and the exploration of spirituality and the divine feminine. These books are recommended if you're interested in exploring these themes more deeply:

Aging and Personal Growth

- **The Second Half of Life:** Opening the Eight Gates of Wisdom by Angeles Arrien explores the challenges and surprises of aging and how to open oneself to the gifts of maturity and wisdom.

- **From Age-ing to Sage-ing:** A Revolutionary Approach to Growing Older by Zalman Schachter-Shalomi offers a spiritual and holistic approach to the issues of aging, providing tools for spiritual growth and community building.

- **Falling Upward:** A Spirituality for the Two Halves of Life by Richard Rohr discusses how the failures and challenges of the first half of life are actually stepping stones to the spiritual richness of the second half.

- **Goddesses Never Age:** The Secret Prescription for Radiance, Vitality, and Well-Being by Christiane Northrup challenges conventional beliefs about aging and demonstrates how to maintain joy, health, and vitality throughout life.

- **Life Reimagined:** The Science, Art, and Opportunity of Midlife by Barbara Bradley Hagerty provides an insightful look into midlife, presenting research and stories that illustrate how these years can be a period of unprecedented growth and fulfillment.

- **The Gift of Years:** Growing Older Gracefully by Joan Chittister examines the many dimensions of aging and argues that it is a time full of opportunities for learning, growth, and understanding the essence of life.

- **This Chair Rocks:** A Manifesto Against Ageism by Ashton Applewhite challenges societal norms about aging, advocating for a shift in perception that reframes aging as an empowering aspect of life.

Divine Feminine and Spirituality

- **The Dance of the Dissident Daughter:** A Woman's Journey from Christian Tradition to the Sacred Feminine by Sue Monk Kidd chronicles the author's journey from a traditional Christian upbringing to discovering the power of the divine feminine within herself.

- **Women Who Run with the Wolves:** Myths and Stories of the Wild Woman Archetype by Clarissa Pinkola Estés is a collection of myths and stories that celebrate the instinctual nature of women, often seen as a foundational work on embracing the wild feminine.

- **Awakening Shakti:** The Transformative Power of the Goddesses of Yoga by Sally Kempton explores the divine feminine energy (Shakti) through the lens of Hindu goddesses, offering practices to awaken these energies within.

- **Goddesses in Everywoman:** Thirtieth Anniversary Edition: Powerful Archetypes in Women's Lives by Jean Shinoda Bolen uses goddess archetypes to explore the dynamics of the feminine psyche, offering insights into personality, relationships, and personal development.

- **The Circle of Life:** The Heart's Journey Through the Seasons by Joyce Rupp and

Macrina Wiederkehr takes readers on a spiritual journey through the seasons of life, emphasizing the cyclical nature of our existence and the lessons each season brings.

- **Sacred Woman:** A Guide to Healing the Feminine Body, Mind, and Spirit by Queen Afua offers a comprehensive spiritual and health guide that reconnects women to their ancestral roots, promoting physical, mental, and spiritual healing.

- **Untie the Strong Woman:** Blessed Mother's Immaculate Love for the Wild Soul by Clarissa Pinkola Estés celebrates the Sacred Mother archetype, exploring how this figure can inspire and empower women to reclaim their strength and spirit.

- **The Book of SHE:** Your Heroine's Journey into the Heart of Feminine Power by Sara Avant Stover guides readers on a journey to embrace their feminine power, weaving together personal stories, exercises, and insights to help women connect with their inner strength.

These books provide a range of perspectives and insights into aging gracefully, embracing personal growth and exploring the depth of spirituality and the divine feminine. Each offers a unique approach to understanding and navigating these complex themes, making them valuable resources for anyone on this journey.

***

To further expand your exploration and understanding of aging gracefully and the crone years, here are additional online resources that offer a diverse range of perspectives, practical advice, and community support for mature women.

Health and Wellness for Aging Women

Prioritizing health and wellness is key to embracing the years with grace, vitality, and strength. From dietary recommendations that cater to changing nutritional needs to engaging in physical activities that enhance mobility and mental health, these resources are designed to support you in maintaining a healthy lifestyle.

- **AARP's Health Section** provides articles, news, and resources on health topics relevant to seniors, including preventive measures, nutrition, fitness, and the management of chronic conditions. Visit AARP Health.

- **Nutrition.gov** offers nutritional guidance and highlights the importance of a healthy diet in supporting brain function, heart health, bone strength, muscle tone, immunity, and mental well-being.

- **The National Institute on Aging** offers practical tips for meal planning, highlighting the value of consuming a variety of foods and staying hydrated. It also provides resources and guidelines for getting started with exercise, emphasizing the importance of choosing activities that are enjoyable and sustainable over the long term.

- **Silver Sneakers** is a fitness program for seniors that offers access to gym memberships, fitness classes, and community events designed to keep older adults physically active and socially engaged.

Creativity, Lifelong Learning, and Engagement

For workshops or online classes in arts, writing, and other creative outlets, consider platforms like Udemy or Coursera. While specific listings vary, these platforms are known for their wide range of creative courses, including art therapy, creative writing, and more. These courses are designed to use creative expression as a tool for self-exploration and personal growth. Searching their course catalog for "creative expression," "art therapy," or "writing workshops" can yield various options tailored to different interests and skill levels.

- **Coursera's Senior Programs** offers online courses from universities and colleges around the world in a wide range of subjects, allowing seniors to continue learning and expanding their knowledge base from the comfort of their home.

- **Road Scholar** is a not-for-profit organization that offers educational tours and learning adventures for adults, focusing on cultural immersion and personal growth.

Additionally, many community centers, local colleges, and wellness centers offer workshops and classes in creative arts. These can be great opportunities to engage with your local community while exploring your creative side.

Financial Planning and Retirement

- **The Motley Fool's Retirement Section** provides financial advice, investment strategies, and retirement planning tips for seniors looking to manage their finances effectively during their golden years.

- **Senior Planet from AARP** focuses on technology and offers resources and articles to help seniors stay updated with the digital world, including online banking, safe internet practices, and social media.

Mindfulness, Spirituality, and Inner Growth

For meditation and mindfulness, apps like Headspace and Calm also offer guided sessions that can be tailored to your needs, including sessions focused on stress reduction, sleep, and the exploration of spirituality. Joining local or online groups dedicated to meditation and creative arts can provide community support and inspiration. Platforms like Meetup often have groups for both meditation and various forms of creative arts.

- **DailyOM** offers courses and articles on spirituality, personal development, and holistic health, with content that can resonate with women in their crone years seeking deeper inner growth and connection.

- **The Wild Woman Project** is a global network focused on women's circles, workshops, and retreats that aim to connect women to their wild, untamed nature and deepen their spiritual journey.

- **Insight Timer** offers a meditation titled "Activating The Divine Feminine," which aims to connect you to your inner strength and nurturing qualities, tapping into deep creativity and openness.

- **S.A.G.E. Holistic Health and Wellness Center** provides insights on finding your inner goddess and honoring the divine feminine within through intentional practices. They suggest creating a goddess sanctuary in your personal space, engaging in rituals to bring sacredness to your life, prioritizing time in nature, and embracing authenticity and vulnerability as a form of strength.

The journey to inner peace and connecting with the divine feminine is personal and unique to each individual. Exploring a variety of practices and activities can help you find what resonates most deeply with you.

Community and Volunteering

If you're interested in volunteer opportunities that emphasize personal growth and community engagement and leverage the wisdom and life experience of mature individuals, several resources stand out. These platforms facilitate connections with organizations seeking volunteers across various sectors, emphasizing the valuable contributions of older adults.

- VolunteerMatch is a versatile platform that connects volunteers with nonprofit organizations based on their interests and location. VolunteerMatch offers a wide range of categories, including opportunities specifically tailored for seniors who wish to contribute their time and skills to causes they care about.

- AARP provides a tool (Volunteer Wizard) to help individuals find volunteering opportunities that match their skills and interests. This resource is particularly focused on opportunities suitable for older adults, ranging from mentoring and tutoring to advocacy and community service.

- Now operating under AmeriCorps, the Corporation for National and Community Service (CNCS) offers a variety of volunteer opportunities nationwide, including the Senior Corps program, which is specifically designed for individuals fifty-five and older. Programs under Senior Corps include Foster Grandparents, Senior Companions, and RSVP (Retired and Senior Volunteer Program), all of which are tailored to fit the interests and capabilities of senior volunteers.

- Idealist is a platform where individuals can find volunteer opportunities, nonprofit jobs, and internships. Idealist allows users to filter searches by interest area, time commitment, and location, making it easier to find suitable volunteer roles across the United States. Visit Idealist.

- Points of Light is a global organization with a network of affiliates across the United States; it offers a variety of volunteer opportunities that cater to different interests, including initiatives specifically designed for older adults. Points of Light also provides resources for individuals looking to start their own community service projects.

- engAGED (The National Resource Center for Engaging Older Adults) is a comprehensive platform dedicated to increasing the social engagement of older adults, people with disabilities, and caregivers. This initiative offers a variety of resources to support organizations in developing and enhancing social engagement programming. It features a range of social engagement innovations, best practices, and tools that can be utilized to foster meaningful community involvement and personal growth through volunteerism.

- Community Awareness Toolkit by engAGED provides materials designed to increase community awareness about the importance of social engagement. The toolkit includes consumer brochures, infographics, fact sheets, and more, all aimed at supporting organizations in their efforts to engage older adults in meaningful activities and volunteer opportunities. These resources are especially valuable for individuals and organizations looking to bridge generational gaps and promote the benefits of social engagement among older adults.

These resources provide a solid foundation for anyone looking to engage in volunteer work that not only benefits older adults but also fosters personal growth and community engagement. Whether your interest lies in direct service, educational roles, or behind-the-scenes support, there are ample opportunities to make a meaningful impact. Engaging in volunteer work can enhance your skill set, expand your social connections, and contribute to a more vibrant and interconnected community. These platforms showcase the diverse ways in which seniors can get involved, share their expertise, and make significant contributions to society, all while fostering personal growth and strengthening community bonds.

***

These resources complement the existing recommendations by providing a broader spectrum of support, information, and community for women navigating the later stages of life. Whether you're seeking to improve your physical health, expand your mind, manage your finances, connect with others, or deepen your spiritual practice, these platforms offer valuable insights and opportunities for engagement.

Embrace the Wisdom

This comprehensive guide was carefully curated to support women navigating the profound journey of aging. Through the diverse array of resources shared—from vibrant online communities and insightful therapy options to enriching self-help literature and extensive online platforms—we aimed to equip you with the tools necessary for a fulfilling transition into the crone years.

Our exploration spanned the essentials of health and wellness, emphasizing the importance of a balanced diet and regular physical activity—critical components in maintaining vitality and well-being. The guide also ventured into the realms of creativity, lifelong learning, and engagement, offering pathways to keep the mind active and the spirit engaged. Financial planning and retirement resources provided practical advice for secure and worry-free golden years, while sections on mindfulness, spirituality, and inner growth invited you to deepen your connection with the divine feminine and harness your inner strength.

Community and volunteering opportunities highlighted the invaluable contributions mature individuals can make, leveraging their wisdom and life experience to foster personal growth and community engagement. These platforms not only allow for meaningful contributions to society but also enhance personal well-being and expand social networks.

This guide is a starting point—a tool to assist you in discovering and accessing the wealth of support available for women in their crone years. It's an invitation to embrace aging not as a decline but as a continuation of life's adventure, rich with opportunities for growth, learning, and fulfillment. Embrace the wisdom of your years, and may you live your crone years to their fullest potential.

Selected Bibliography

Arrien, Angeles. *The Four-Fold Way: Walking the Paths of the Warrior,* Teacher, *Healer and Visionary.* New York: HarperCollins, 1993.

Bateson, Mary Catherine. *Composing a Life.* New York: Atlantic Monthly Press, 1989.

Bolen, Jean Shinoda. *Close to the Bone: Life-threatening Illness and the Search for Meaning.* New York: Scribner, 1996, Simon & Schuster, 1997.

Goddesses in Older Women: Archetypes in Women Over Fifty. New York: HarperCollins, 2001.

The Millionth Circle: How to Change Ourselves and the World. Berkeley: Conari Press, 1999.

Castaneda, Carlos. *The Teachings of Don Juan: A Yaqui Way of Knowledge.* New York: Simon & Schuster, 1974.

Eliot, T. S. "The Dry Salvages" in *Four Quartets.* New York: Harcourt, Brace and Company, 1943.

Han, Thich Nhat. *Peace Is Every Step: The Path of Mindfulness in Everyday Life.* New York: Bantam Books, 1992.

Heilbrun, Carolyn G. *The Last Gift of Time: Life Beyond Sixty.* New York: Dial Press, 1997.

Steinem, Gloria. "Doing Sixty" in *Moving Beyond Words.* New York: Simon & Schuster, 1994.

Mango Publishing, established in 2014, publishes an eclectic list of books by diverse authors—both new and established voices—on topics ranging from business, personal growth, women's empowerment, LGBTQ studies, health, and spirituality to history, popular culture, time management, decluttering, lifestyle, mental wellness, aging, and sustainable living. We were recently named 2019 and 2020's #1 fastest growing independent publisher by *Publishers Weekly*. Our success is driven by our main goal, which is to publish high quality books that will entertain readers as well as make a positive difference in their lives.

Our readers are our most important resource; we value your input, suggestions, and ideas. We'd love to hear from you—after all, we are publishing books for you!

Please stay in touch with us and follow us at:
    Facebook: Mango Publishing
    Twitter: @MangoPublishing
    Instagram: @MangoPublishing
    LinkedIn: Mango Publishing
    Pinterest: Mango Publishing
    Newsletter: mangopublishinggroup.com/newsletter

Join us on Mango's journey to reinvent publishing, one book at a time.